Special thanks to
Fukui Prefectural Dinosaur Museum

First US edition 2023
First published by Berbay Publishing (Australia) 2022

Library of Congress Catalog Card Number 2022908177
ISBN 978-1-5362-3069-7

23 24 25 26 27 28 APS 10 9 8 7 6 5 4 3 2 1

Printed in Humen, Dongguan, China

This book was typeset in Futura.
The illustrations were done in cut paper.

Candlewick Studio
an imprint of
Candlewick Press
99 Dover Street
Somerville, Massachusetts 02144

www.candlewickstudio.com

Whose Dinosaur Bones Are Those?

Chihiro Takeuchi

CANDLEWICK STUDIO
an imprint of Candlewick Press

WHOSE
DINOSAUR BONES?

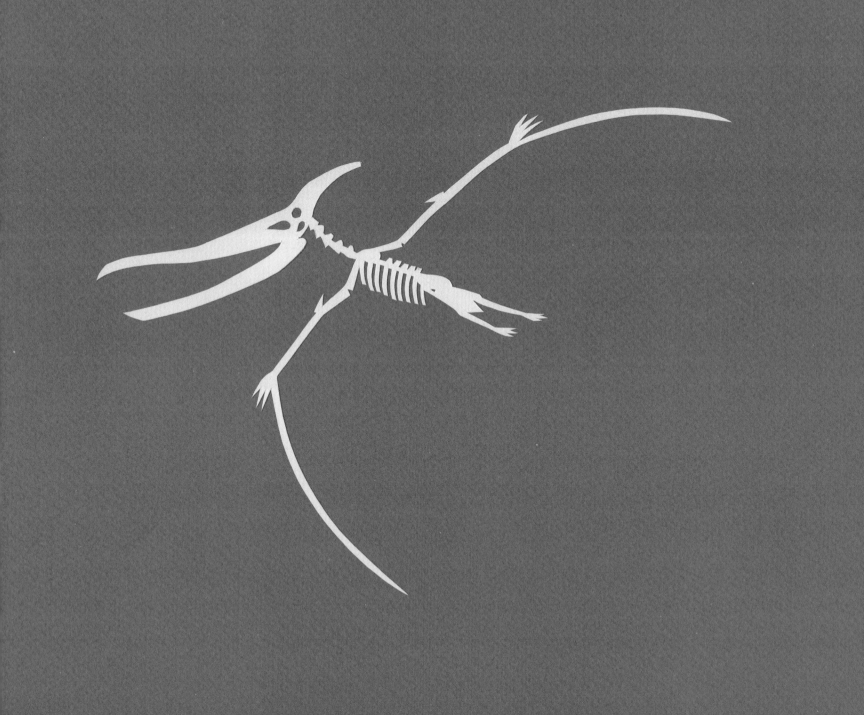

A Pteranodon!

WHOSE
DINOSAUR BONES?

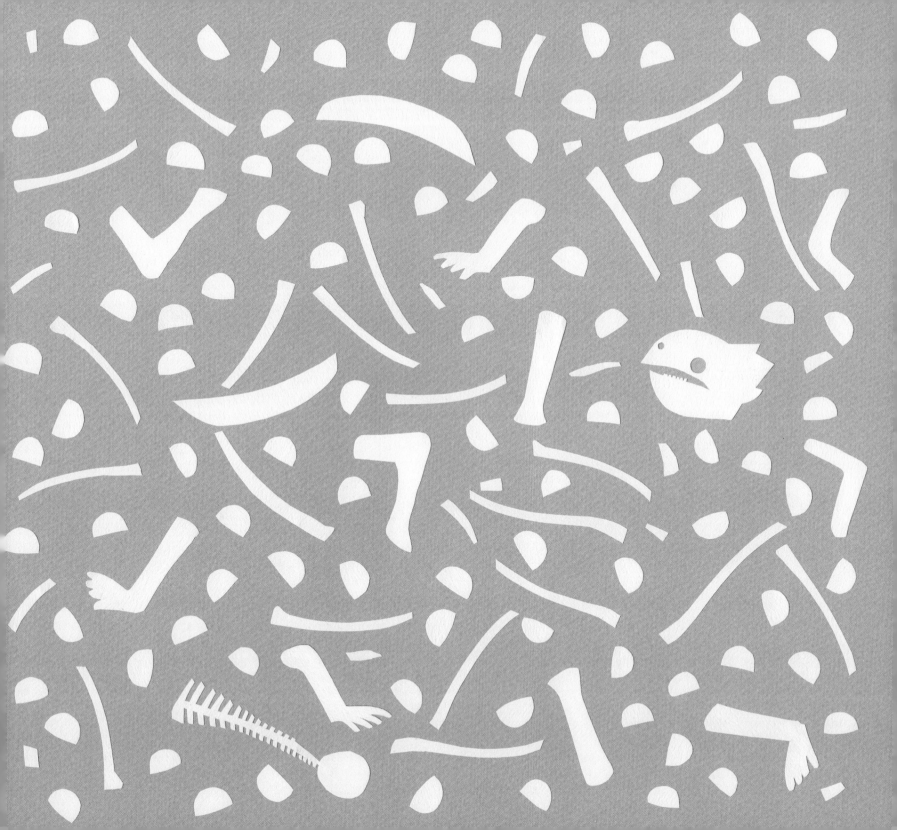

An Ankylosaurus!

WHOSE
DINOSAUR BONES?

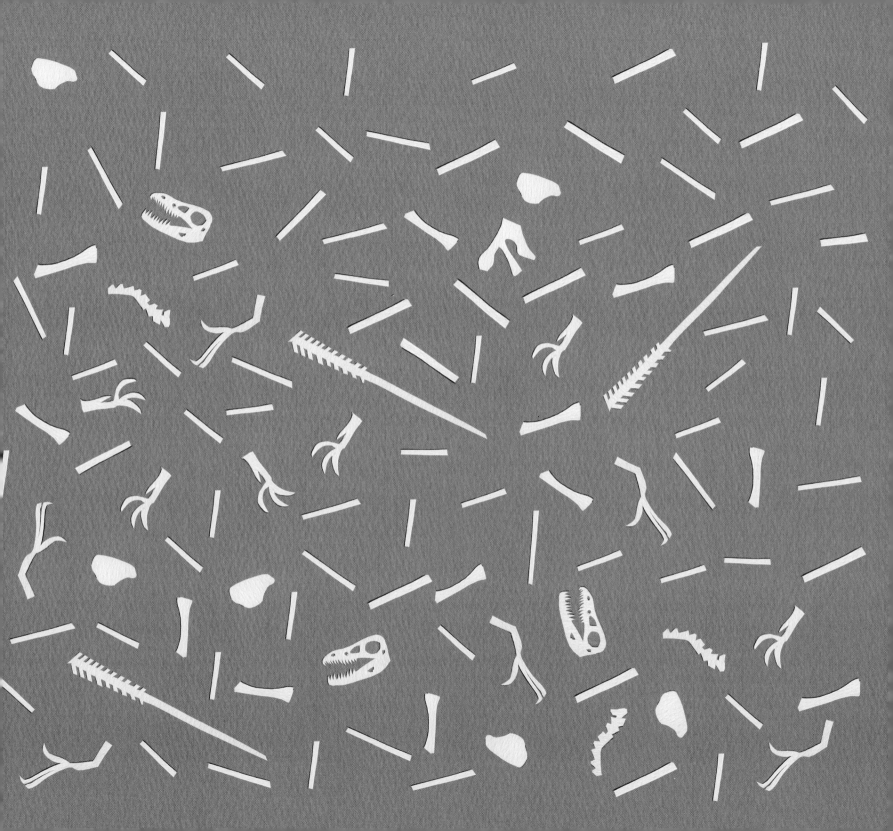

Velociraptors!

WHOSE
DINOSAUR BONES?

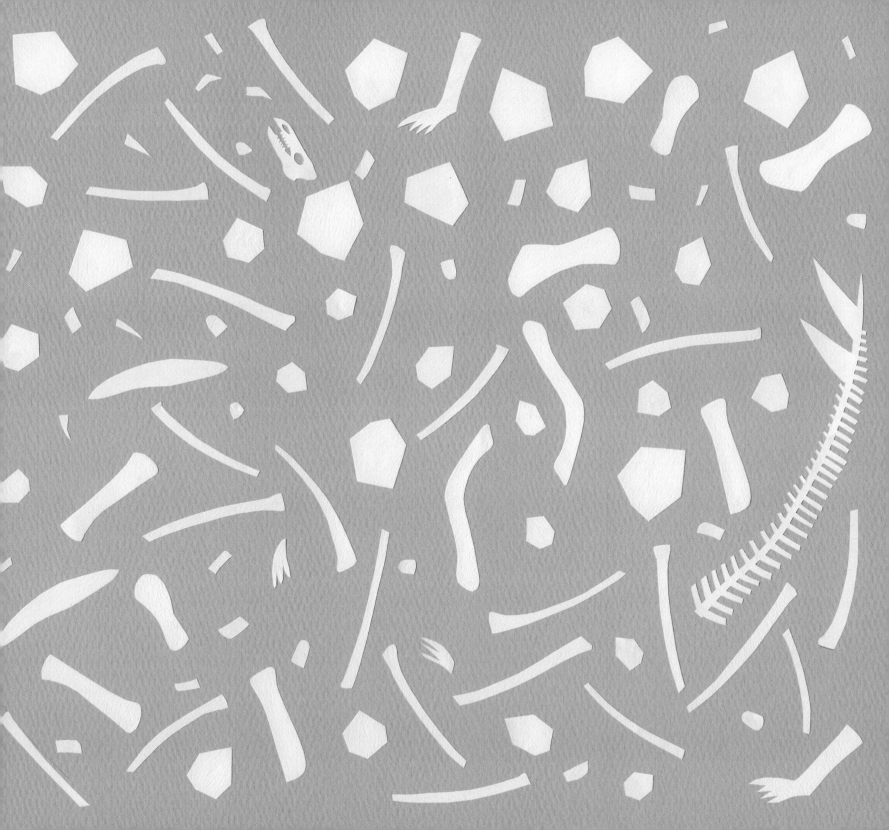

A Stegosaurus!

WHOSE
DINOSAUR BONES?

A Mosasaurus!

WHOSE DINOSAUR BONES?

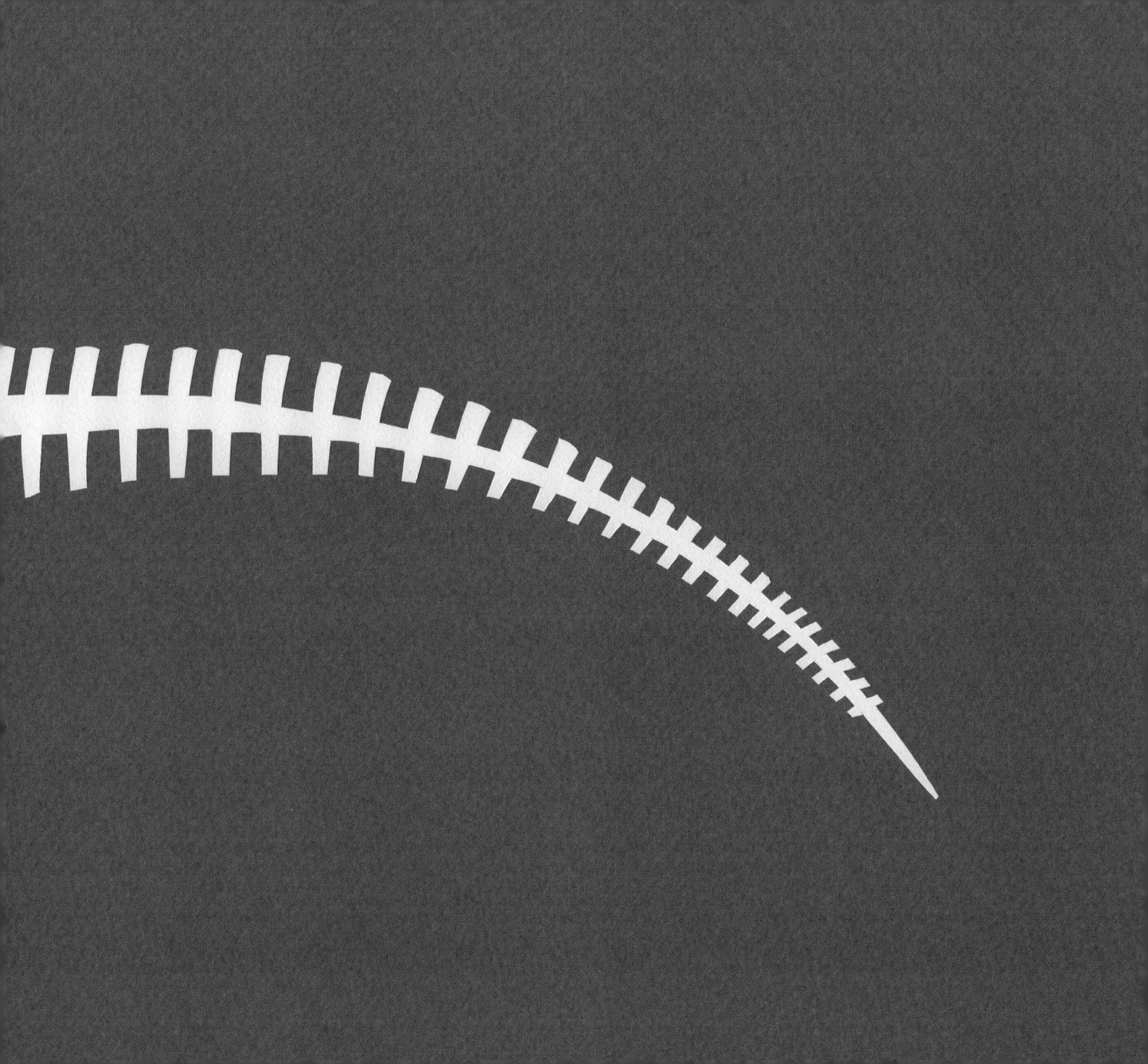

A Tyrannosaurus!

WHOSE DINOSAUR BONES?

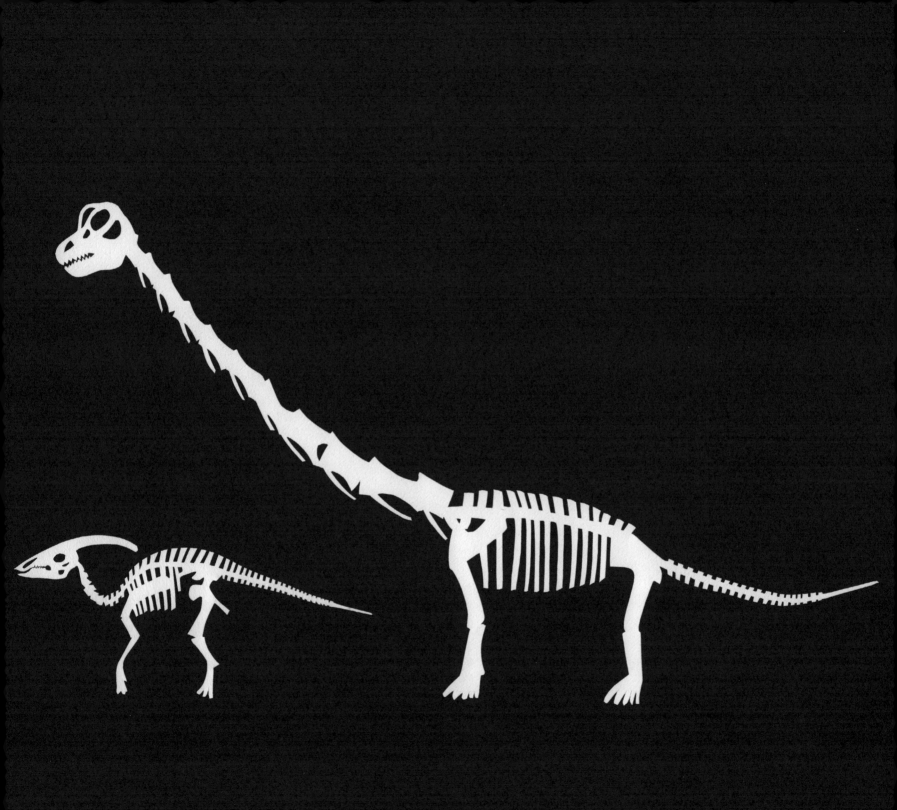

A Spinosaurus!

An Allosaurus!

A Brachiosaurus!

A Parasaurus!

FUN FACTS

Did you know that Pteranodon is not really a dinosaur? It's a closely related flying reptile called a Pterosaur.

Did you know that Ankylosaurus was a tanklike dinosaur? It was covered in plates that protected it like armor.

Did you know that Velociraptor had deadly sickle claws on its legs?

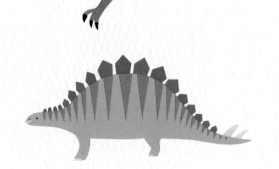

Did you know that the plates on Stegosaurus were attached to its skin, not its skeleton?

Did you know that, like Pteranodon, Mosasaurus was not a dinosaur? It was a dangerous water reptile, much like a crocodile.

Did you know that a Tyrannosaurus tooth is about 8 inches (20 centimeters) long?

Did you know that Spinosaurus was the largest carnivorous dinosaur? It was even bigger than Tyrannosaurus.

Did you know that an average-size Allosaurus weighed about as much as a car?

Did you know that Brachiosaurus had longer front legs than back legs? This helped it to reach leaves on tall trees.